Help with high impact presentations

by David Lancaster and Julian Janes

Authors' Background

David and Julian are providers of "High Impact" Presentation Skills training.

Their background is unique. They are former Royal Navy training officers whose job was to provide an "in-house" consultancy service to the middle and senior ranking RN/MOD personnel who regularly gave presentations to:

- The Prime Minister
- Members of Cabinet
- Government & Civil Service Committees
- National & International Conferences
- Television & Radio Briefings

The task involved message design, script writing, personal coaching and general advice. These presentations and briefings had to be highly professional, persuasive and, above all, sell ideas and concepts to a very critical audience.

They left the Navy in 1989 to set up Presentation Techniques Ltd and now regularly provide a similar service to over 50 Blue Chip companies, investment banks and consultancies, with whom they have developed close relationships.

Their no-nonsense, direct approach and application of advanced techniques has proved to be extremely popular with Managers and Directors across the commercial world. Comments from some of them can be seen in this book.

The Book

This book is the result of intensive research and experience gained from operating in stressful and highly demanding environments.

As it is designed to be an 'easy read', we have tried to keep it as short as possible. Theory is only included where absolutely necessary in order to understand its practical application.

There are 7 chapters:

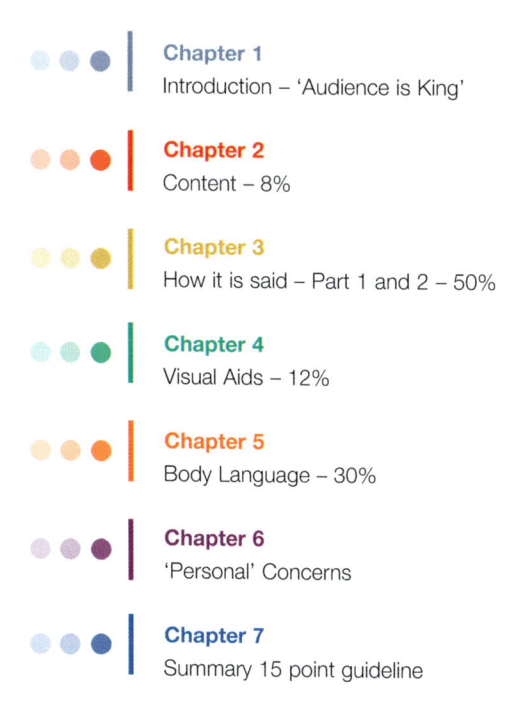

Chapter 1
Introduction – 'Audience is King'

Chapter 2
Content – 8%

Chapter 3
How it is said – Part 1 and 2 – 50%

Chapter 4
Visual Aids – 12%

Chapter 5
Body Language – 30%

Chapter 6
'Personal' Concerns

Chapter 7
Summary 15 point guideline

Chapter 1
Audience is King!

At the start of one of our courses, a senior manager asked us what we thought of his presentation. As he had delivered the same presentation a month previously to his board, we asked how it had gone at the time and whether he had got what he intended. His reply provides a salutary lesson:

"NO! They kept interrupting me! I never got to say what I'd intended – I think they were just being bloody-minded!

Audiences have an uncanny knack. They seem to have their own agendas and, despite the best preparation, will always dictate that things never go according to plan. Or so it seems.

In reality, the cause of this very common malaise is nothing to do with the audience at all. It is almost always entirely the fault of the presenter.

We try to provide all the people we train with a simple philosophy: the presenter is irrelevant; the audience is king. The reasons for this seemingly brutal approach should be obvious. If the audience says "it's a good presentation", it is a good presentation. If an audience says you are a good presenter, you are a good presenter. The case for reversing this theory would indeed be a challenge to present!

The problems described by our manager stem from a fundamental flaw in the way that the vast majority of people communicate. Most people follow the simple model described in figure 1. It is know as 'Egocentric communication'.

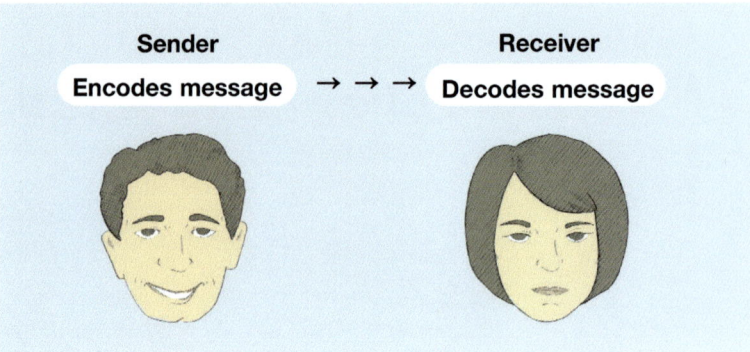

Figure 1

In this model, the sender (the presenter) decides what he wants to say and the way he is going to say it, then sends it to the receiver (the audience). Their job is hard work. They try to decode the original message in terms which they can relate to.

Two things happen. Either the message is misinterpreted, and/or it is changed, filtered or edited so as to fit into a pre-conceived framework in the mind of the listener. The term 'egocentric' applies in this case because of the emphasis this model gives to the presenter: 'I (presenter) have decided what I (presenter) want to say and the way I (presenter) am going to say it.

I (presenter) then say it and I (presenter) assume that you (audience) will get the message in more or less the way I (presenter) intended it to be'.

Anyone remembering the classic game of Chinese whispers, where an oral message passed from person to person breaks down very rapidly, will know the problems caused by this model of communication! It is no use blaming the listening skills involved – that would be blaming the audience – and that is never a wise thing to do! In presentation terms, it results in the classic 'low-impact' presentation so often suffered by business audiences.

Help with **High Impact Presentations** | 7

So, what do the professional communicators do to address this problem?

The answer is that they add a vital third phase into the model, as shown below. This is known as 'translated message' communication.

Remember!

- It's not what you say, it's the way that you say it...

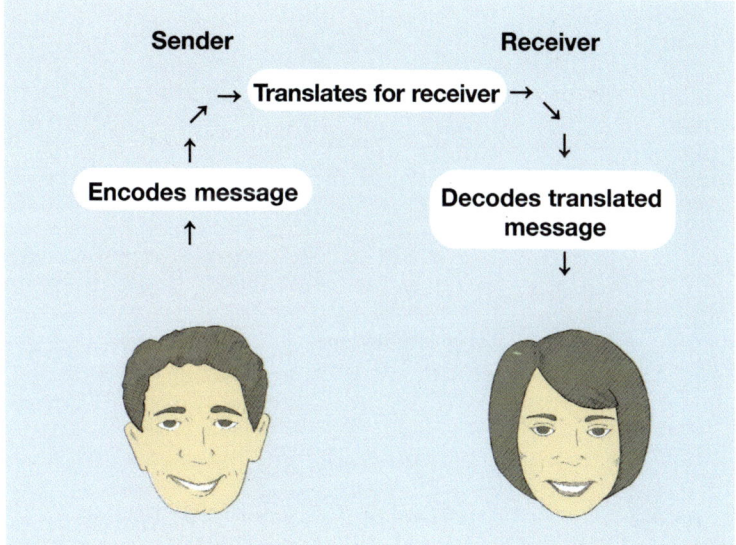

Figure 2

In this model, the sender encodes a message as before, ie decides what they want to say but then moves into translation phase and takes account of a whole series of issues from the audience's point of view. The effect is to package the message in terms that suit the receiver and then release a far more relevant and penetrating version for the audience or receiver to decode. When done correctly, the result is the dreamed of 'high-impact' presentations which most speakers secretly crave for – not to mention audiences!
This book explains the techniques used to ensure successful translation and, therefore, impactful presentations.

A good starting point is to examine the results of many surveys conducted on sample audiences listening to presentations and what makes an impact on them.

The one we use as the basis for our training is certainly reinforced by our experience and shows the following breakdown during a presentation:

50%	**How it is said**
30%	**Body language**
12%	**Visual aids**
8%	**Content**

It is worth noting here that other surveys have produced slight variations on this theme, but that there is never any disagreement on the fact that pure content is not highly rated! Strangely enough, most 'egocentric' communicators seem to find this fact alarming and usually ignore it. Audiences do not like listening to pure content! Remember: 'The Audience is King'.

The rest of this book uses the breakdown above as the basis for a concise, practical, step-by-step guide for producing and delivering high-impact presentations. The intention is that, by working quickly through each chapter in turn, you will gradually develop your presentation. In short, it tries to highlight what professional communicators do when presenting.
Remember the famous maxim:

"....It's not what you say, it's the way that you say it...."

Ask yourself this question....what are you trying to achieve with your presentation? In the words of George Bernard Shaw, "We are all in the business of selling". Whether you are selling your ideas, your products or your business, in order to do so, you must first sell yourself.

To do that, you must create the right impression.

Chapter 2
Content (8%)

Imagine a human being. What do you see? You see flesh covering muscles, ligaments, tissue etc. What you do not see is the skeleton – the essential bone structure or framework that holds everything in place. This principle should also be applied to the design of presentations. The skeleton in this case is the content – the bones of the message, the things you need the audience to remember.

We have devised a simple method of ensuring that you get the correct points across every time, whilst pure content is kept in its rightful place! If you do not adopt this approach from the beginning, you will end up with a jumble of words that will mean the audience has to do all the work. They will not – it is up to you to do it for them.

The first thing to decide is the 'Aim' of your presentation. In other words, what do you want to achieve from it?

Imagine this as a journey. The aim is the final destination. In the same way that you could not end up in two places at once at the end of your journey, you cannot do this with a presentation either. There are three tests of an aim statement:

- **Is it honestly what you want?**
- **Is it singular?**
- **Is it short and to the point?**

With the above in mind, there are only two things a presentation can achieve. It can convince or persuade, or it can give an understanding. It is fair to say that the great majority of business presentations are intended to convince or persuade. The number of times, however, that we have had to forcibly point this out to the people we train is staggering. What we often hear is: 'I want to brief them on the latest expenditure plans.' What was really meant was, 'I want them to increase my budget by £250,000!' Always remember test number one – is it honestly what you want!

So, how should these aim statements be expressed? If you follow ONE of the wordings below, you will not go far wrong:

> 'To give you an understanding of...'

Or

> 'To convince you to...'

All you then need to do is literally finish the sentence off, eg:

> 'To give you an understanding of the latest developments in the "city centre project".'

> 'To convince you of the need to change our short-term strategy.'

Once you have decided your aim and written it down as a sentence, you can proceed to stage two – deciding the Vital Points'.

These are the major issues you will have to address in order to achieve your aim. They are the points you head for on each leg of your journey. The question is, how do you decide these and how many should there be? Before you can answer that question you need to understand how to analyse your intended audience in a way that will help you design your message.

We use a very basic, yet accurate, model to help us do this. It is one of many such models authored by psychologists. We decide the answers to three questions:

- **What character types are we dealing with?**
- **How can we recognise them in advance?**
- **What happens when we have a mixture?**

We will deal with questions 1 and 2 first. The model we use is detailed below:

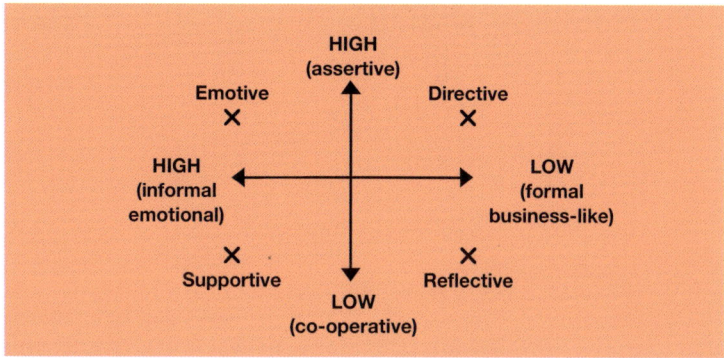

Figure 3

The vertical line shows levels of dominance, the horizontal line, levels of sociability. The idea is to judge which 'box' your intended audience falls into.

We will look at each one in turn, starting with the **'EMOTIVE'**. These people are high in dominance and high in sociability. What sort of people are they?

- Sociable
- Spontaneous
- Zestful
- Stimulating
- Emotional
- Unstructured
- Excitable
- Personable
- Dynamic

These are the 'people-oriented' people who are animated and constantly introducing change into their lives. They also have a short attention span. They prefer a general picture and dislike details intensely. So, when presenting to them, **keep it short and sweet and try to cover the points in an interesting and 'broad brush' manner.**

The second character type the model describes is the **'DIRECTIVE'** – high in dominance but low in sociability. These people come across as:

- Aggressive
- Intense
- Requiring
- Pushy
- Serious
- Determined
- Frank
- Opinionated
- Bold

Remember!

- Give them the facts and nothing but the facts.

They often give the impression they don't like people. This is because they are goal-driven. They separate work and pleasure and, when at work, will often cut through resistance (human or bureaucratic) to achieve their aims. When presenting to these people, **give them the facts and nothing but the facts. Get to the point, cover it clinically and move on.**

The third character type is the **'REFLECTIVE'**. These people are low in both dominance and sociability. They are:

- Precise
- Deliberate
- Questioning
- Aloof
- Scientific
- Pre-occupied
- Serious
- Stuffy

They are often the product people, the scientists and engineers, whose jobs involve the attention to detail that other types will avoid. The same applies when they are listening to presentations – they are looking for all the detail. So, **give them the details.** Support statements with information, try to address their questioning approach by lengthening your presentation to include a much closer look at the subject than that required by Emotives and Directives.

The final character type is the **'SUPPORTIVE'** – high in sociability, low in dominance. They are easy to recognise:

- Loyal
- Steady
- Solid
- Reliable
- Good workers

These people form the majority of most populations – the backbone of the nation. When presenting to Supportives, it must be remembered that they do not respond well to change and will worry if given cause. The message, therefore, has to be reassuring. It must take into account their concerns and not come across as uncaring or aggressive. Take time to ensure you cover points fully and gently. Always try to pre-empt any contentious issues and show that they can be dealt with.

It is important to identify which characters you are presenting to in advance (speak to secretaries, people who know them, look at their position, age etc) and then change your message to match your analysis.
In summary:

EMOTIVES	-	general picture
DIRECTIVES	-	facts
REFLECTIVES	-	details
SUPPORTIVES	-	reassurance

That leaves the final, and by now, obvious question – what happens when you are faced with a mixed audience?

There are three possible scenarios. Firstly, let us take a situation where you are faced with a large audience, say 30 plus. They will have a common thread and you can use this to make a common-sense decision, based on your assessment of which character forms the majority. For example, a gathering of sales and marketing personnel is likely to be mainly Emotives – so you would give them a general picture. A group of senior managers/directors is more often than not going to contain a majority of Directives – so you would present the facts. Groups of engineers on mass tend to be largely Reflectives – so they would need detail. And finally, a gathering of shop-floor employees will be mainly Supportives – so a reassuring style would be required.

The second scenario for a mixed audience is a smaller one like the one shown in Figure 4.

Figure 4

In this case, you need to ask yourself one question. Is there a key person/decision-maker who will influence the rest? If there is, hit him/her, ie design your presentation to suit that particular person's need.

The final possible scenario is again a small group as in Figure 4, but with no key decision-maker. This is the trickiest situation of all. Our advice here is to design a DIRECTIVE presentation. The reason for this is that the EMOTIVE will be generally happy because at least you have been 'punchy and to the point'. The DIRECTIVE will certainly be happy. The REFLECTIVE will require more detail so make sure you back your presentation with handouts that contain additional expansion of the points you made. The SUPPORTIVE will be influenced by the others during the presentation and can be spoken to before and afterwards to address any specific concerns they will have – very rarely are they in positions of power.

As a final point, and to illustrate how this works in reality, we were approached a number of years ago by a well-known sports retailing chain.

Every year they had been staging a major conference, drawing together all their Store, Area and Regional Management teams. They were spending a lot of money on the usual paraphernalia and still receiving poor feedback. We asked them to profile their audience. They told us they tried to employ young, sporty, outgoing types in order to portray the right image for their products. We were able to agree that the majority of the audience would therefore be Emotives. They had been subjecting this group to seven hours plus of cost analysis, sales figures, projections and so on and had, in short, clearly been boring them to tears! We got the board to cut the conference to half a day. We then designed motivational, 'general picture' style presentations for them to deliver. The result was tremendous feedback and a halving of costs to boot!

What is your audience profile?

- Are they......
- Or are they......

Why had it been going so wrong in the past? The Managing Director was an accountant by background and very Reflective. He thought it was important to give all the details because it was what **he** would have wanted. A classic case of the 'Egocentric' communication mentioned in Chapter One! You cannot and should not beat your head against the brick wall of the audience. Remember, everyone has different ways of taking information in and there is nothing sinister about that fact. **You** need to change **your** message to suit **them**, not the other way round!

Having explained the model and its practical application, we can now return to the Aim sentence and to the task of deciding the vital points.

The method we advise is stunningly simple. It will ensure that the vital points are properly targeted and, more importantly, non-egocentric. What you need to do, having decided the audience type from the model previously described, is approach people who belong to the **same character group** as your audience. Ask them the following question: "What would you need to know which would…." (and then read your Aim out to them). To use one of the Aims we gave as an earlier example: "What would you need to know which would convince you of the need to change our short-term strategy?" They will reply, usually, with a series of questions: for example:

"Okay – firstly, what are the problems with the current strategy? Then, how can we solve them? Are there any disadvantages?, and, what would the benefits be?"

This will then produce 4 vital points for you to cover in the allotted time (Chapter 3 explains time allocation). If you were not happy with these points, you would simply repeat the exercise with another person and merge the two responses.

The great benefit of this system is its speed. People normally spend hours sifting through information, trying to decide what to use, then editing down into manageable chucks of information. Why? The system we use means you know exactly what to cover and, therefore, what information to gather – and it takes 30 seconds to ascertain! Another very significant point will emerge. What you think is important quite often is not and, conversely, what you had not thought of as relevant, quite often is! As we have already said, these points will be 'non-egocentric' – they will, by definition, be what the **audience** wants to hear – not what you want to tell them.

Before we explain what to do next, it is necessary to mention something about the methods of delivery.

You have three options. You could memorise your presentation. This is totally unnecessary unless you present the same subject day in, day out. The reason for not bothering to memorise your presentation is simple. It takes too much time, too much effort, and usually results in a stilted style of delivery because you have to concentrate so hard on **what** to say rather than **how** to say it.

The second option is to write a full script and read from it. Our advice is – DON'T! Unless you have access to a professional speechwriter and you have been trained, like an actor, to deliver pre-determined words, you will sound dreadful. How many times have you witnessed people at conferences, reading from autocues/text and thought they sounded dull and boring? Not to mention the loss of eye-contact and restriction on voice projection this causes.

Tip:

- Try to use free, conversational speech, using some form of notes to jog your memory. The results are always refreshing…

Thus, for the reasons we, in common it has to be said with a lot of professionals in our field, recommend the use of 'extemporaneous' speech. This is simply free, conversational speech, using some form of notes to jog your memory. Without any doubt at all, the results are always refreshing.

The speaker sounds natural, normal and spontaneous. It takes a bit of confidence but it is true to say that we have yet to see one person, in all our years of training, who is incapable of pulling this off.

> **So:**
> **SPEAK FREELY, USING BRIEF NOTES TO SPARK OFF YOUR THOUGHTS.**

Having side-tracked slightly to explain the idea of speaking from notes, we can now return to the example we are using to demonstrate how to put together the content of your presentation:

> **Aim:**
> - To convince you of the need to change our short-term strategy
>
> **Vital Points:**
> - What are the problems with the current strategy?
> - How can we solve them?
> - Are there any disadvantages?
> - What would the benefits be?

The next stage is to start preparing the speaker notes. Use A4 paper or, if the audience you are addressing is in excess of 20, 8 x 5 record cards. (This is the best size to use for larger audiences because the cards are not too big to hold but are big enough to contain a reasonable amount of information and allow you to move around as you speak. Use one side only and keep them separate – do not 'tag' them together – this causes unnecessary problems as you delivery the presentation.

Take one sheet or card per vital point and write each point at the top of each card in a box (see example below):

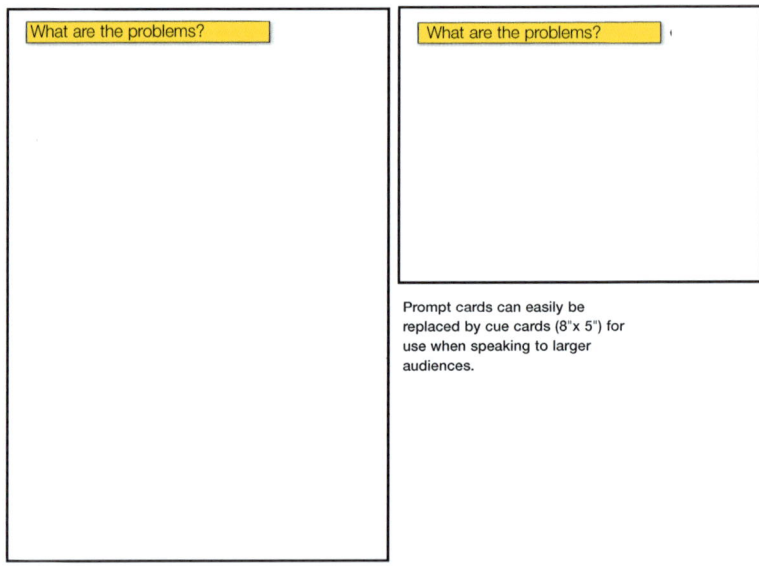

Figure 5

Next take a step back and ask yourself, 'What areas do I need to cover to **answer the question?**' These will become the final part of the content – what we call the 'Bullet Points'. These must be answers to the question. Test each proposed answer using the 'so what?' method. For example, answering the question – What are the problems? with 'unhappy sales staff' would fail this test. Why? Because 'unhappy sales staff' means poor performance. Poor performance means loss of potential business. Therefore the answer which passes the 'so what?' test, **should** be, **"We're losing business".** When you have decided these, add them in boxes down the left-hand side of the speaker notes, leaving spaces in between for later development. To use our first vital point as an example:

Help with **High Impact Presentations** | 21

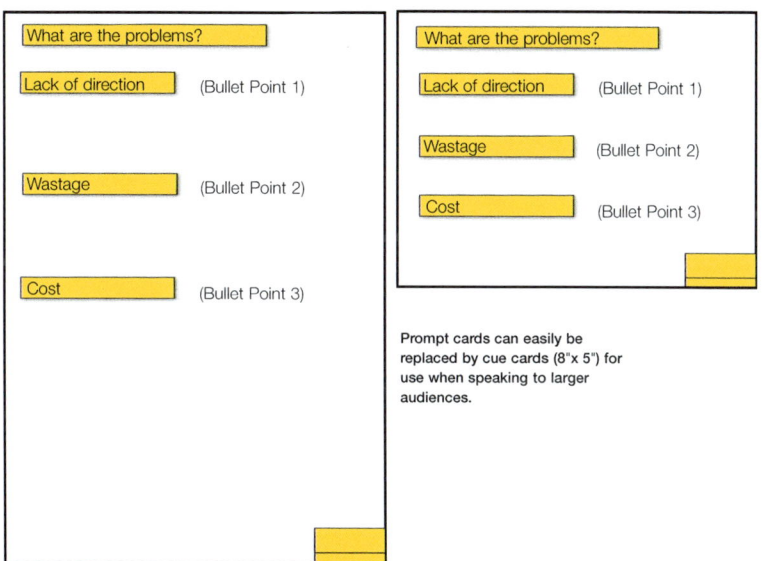

Figure 6

You need to continue with this principle for the other Vital Points until each card or sheet looks similar to the example in Figure 6. Do not put more than 3 bullets per sheet or card. If you need more space (there may for example be 5 bullet points), simply insert another card and continue as before, with bullet points down the left-hand side, in boxes. The reason we advocate boxes will be clearer later in the book – they are a very important feature.

If you have got to this stage correctly, you will have created what we call our 'coffee-filter' principle – explained schematically below:

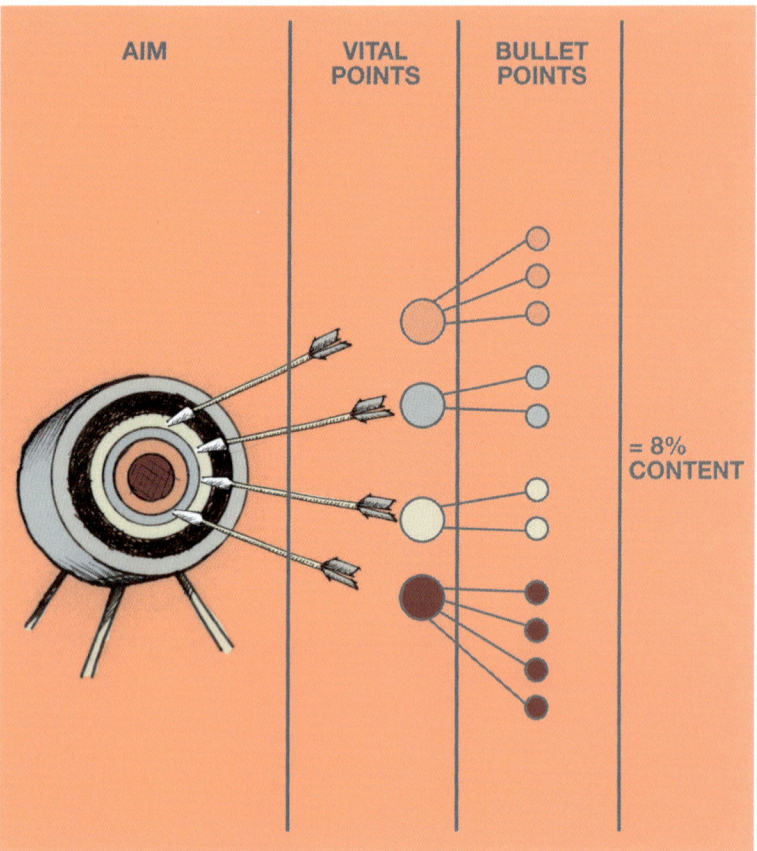

Figure 7

The idea is to achieve your aim. You can think of this as a target. To achieve your target you need the audience to remember clearly the points you make. The Vital Points (the issues they raise) are your means of hitting that target.

The Bullet Points are the areas you will cover to support each Vital Point, which in turn will contribute to your goal – your Aim.

Taken together, all of the above makes up the definition of the word 'content' – the 8% of the impression made on an audience during a presentation.

The next question is: How do you put all of this across in an impactful way? That leads us on to the next section – Chapter 3 – 'How it is said'.

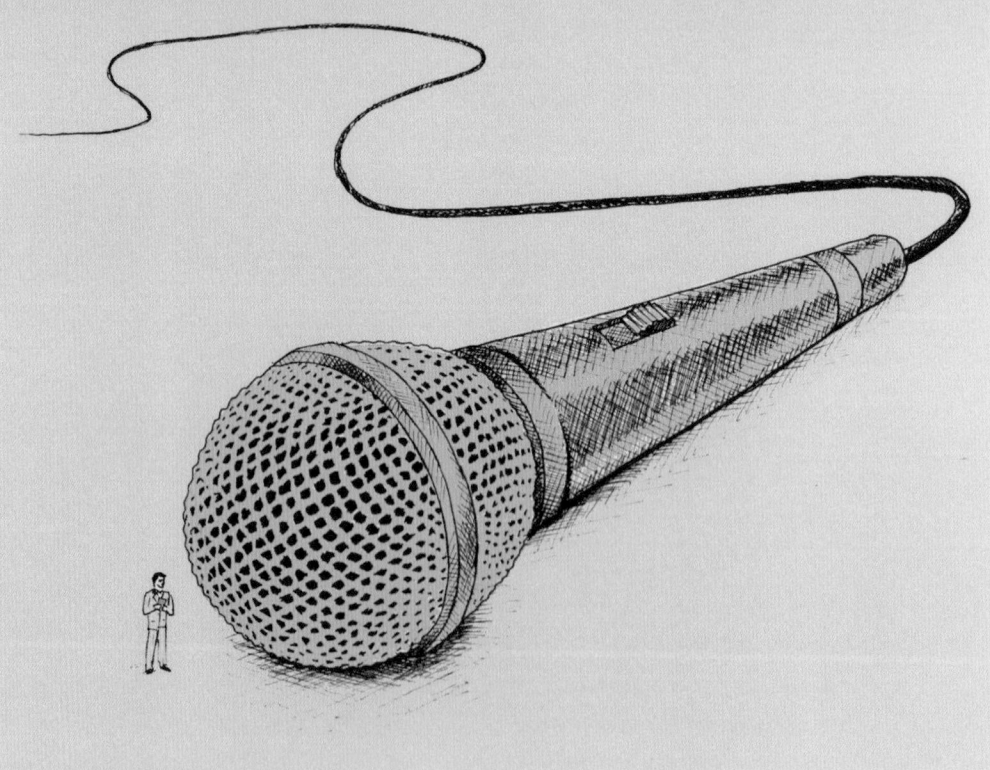

Pricewaterhouse Coopers

"We delivered the presentation to an audience of 60 which was very well received and infinitely better for having seen you last week."

Chapter 3
How It Is Said (50%)

'How it is said' is a combination of 1) message design and 2) the use of the voice. This chapter will look at design first (Part 1) before moving on to voice use (Part 2).

PART 1 – Message Design

A presentation should consist of 3 clearly identifiable parts:

- Introduction
- Main Body
- Conclusion

It has been said that the secret of a good presentation is to "get a good start, get a good finish and get them close together!" This is extremely good advice.

A presentation should consist of 3 clearly identifiable parts – Introduction, Main Body and Conclusion. When asked by delegates on our courses which one of these is the most important, we throw it back at them and ask them to consider the answer for themselves, ie from the audience's point of view. The answer inevitably emerges as a debate between the Introduction and the Conclusion. The fact is that **both** are **equally** the most important parts of the presentation.

The state of mind of most audiences at the start of a presentation can best be described in two words: 'morbid fascination'. 'Morbid' because they are wondering how long it will be, whether it will be interesting and worthwhile – and when they can have a break or even leave altogether! 'Fascination' because they want to see how the presenter will fare and may, hopefully, have interest in the topic to be covered.

The following graph depicts the level of attention over time of a standard, low-impact presentation.

26 | Help with **High Impact Presentations**

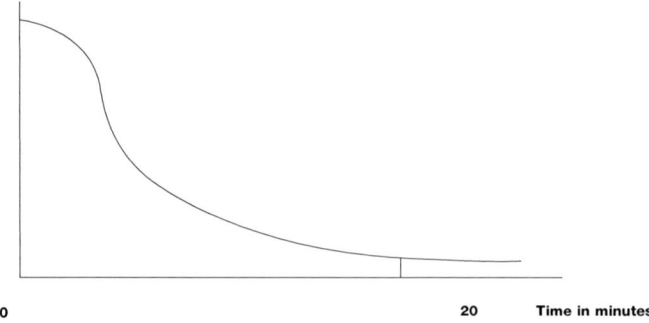

Figure 8

If the start does not 'kill' the morbidity, then, like cancer, it spreads over time, causing the attention to drop rapidly and, what is worse, uneventfully!

Any psychologist will confirm that the bottoming-out comes at minute 20 for an adult audience. However, recent surveys on senior managers and directors show an average attention span of just 10 minutes. They have a lot of other things on their minds – speakers beware!

Good presenters use techniques to tackle these problems. Figure 9 shows the profile of a 'high-impact' presentation. Compare it with Figure 8 and the difference is obvious.

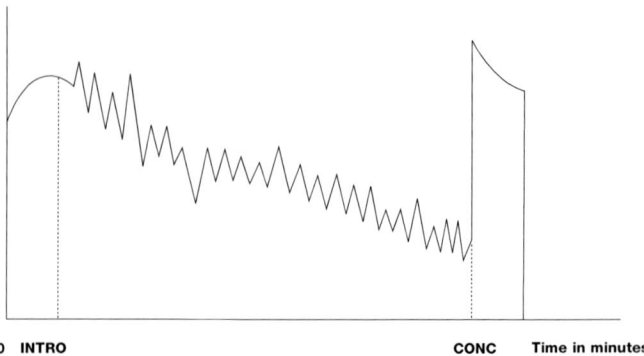

Figure 9

You will notice that attention is raised in the introduction, constantly 'spiked' during the Main Body and hugely raised again for the Conclusion. The overall trend in the middle is still downwards – no-one can halt the fatigue of listening! The reason for the leap at the end is that, when the audience hears the magical words "So, in conclusion....", two things happen. Firstly, they realise that release is close and secondly, because of the relatively low levels of attention towards the middle and end, they pick up and listen more to the Conclusion to make sure they take away the important points.

A good guide for the breakdown of the 3 parts is the 10/80/10 rule. This says, for example, that a 10 minute presentation would have a 1 minute Introduction, an 8 minute Main Body and a 1 minute Conclusion. This rule brings two main advantages:

Remember!

- Get a good start, get a good finish and get them close together!

- **It is a good planning tool**
- **It has the right proportion as far as the audience is concerned**

It should be applied for any length of presentation.
The 'running order' for putting together a presentation is:

- **Main Body**
- **Introduction**
- **Conclusion**

The reason for this will be obvious as we go through each stage – the idea is to speed up preparation.

Main Body (80% of the speaking time)

The first thing to do is arrange the Vital Points into a sequence that will satisfy the audience's needs. This means that the most important point to them comes first and so on, in descending order of importance. If you do not do this, their attention will drop. For example, if "What will it cost?" was a Vital Point and you leave that until the end because you wanted to develop your case – but it was an important factor to them, they will probably:

a   switch off until you cover it
or
b   ask you to cover it first!

Yet again, you must think audience. So, shuffle your cards to get them in the correct sequence.

The second task is to allocate time to each Vital Point. If you use the 10/80/10 principle we mentioned earlier, you will know precisely how long the Main Body is. You now need to say to yourself, "I know the total length of the Main Body (say 8 minutes); how much time am I going to spend on each point?" You might decide on a 3/3/1/1 breakdown, or simply a 2/2/2/2, but you have to make this decision now because it obviously affects how much you can say on each point. If you do not do this, the presentation will overrun or you will end up trying to cut information out later. This is best avoided because, at that stage, you will have established a train of thought that will probably be difficult to disrupt.

In summary, shuffle the cards into the sequence you have decided and allocate speaking time to each one.

We can now move on to look at the rest of this section, developing the Vital Points and Bullet Points we have already established in a way that will be impactful when it is spoken. The first rule is: do not attempt to put in any **more** content. Our task is to get the audience to **remember** the Vital Points and their Bullet Point support, so to do this, we have to move away from pure, undiluted information towards 'design' of messages. You will need to be careful to bear this constantly in mind during the next phase – it is very easy to slip back into bad habits by adding more information. If you do, you will end up with a dull, low-impact presentation.

The next phase we referred to above is to apply what we call the 'tricks of the trade'. These are technically known as 'rhetorical devices' and are the techniques used by professionals to put across their messages. These are the things that cause the 'spikes' in attention levels, particularly during the Main Body (see Figure 9).

The intention here is to provide you with a menu of some of these techniques to choose from. Once we have explained them, we will illustrate how they could be used further to develop the example Vital Point in Chapter 2 – 'What are the problems?'

Here are some of the 'tricks of the trade':

Vivid Language:
This is the technique of painting pictures with words. It is effective because that is how most people recall information.

> **Example 1:**
> "A trillion dollars is the Empire State Building filled from the basement to the top, with dollar bills". (Ronald Reagan)

> **Example 2:**
> "I have seen the Prime Minister and Mr Blair slicing each other up, face to face, against the den of cheers and jeers". (Bill Clinton)

> **Example 3:**
> "A rainbow nation, at peace with itself and the world". (Nelson Mandela, inauguration speech)

Referring to 3rd parties:
This is used to add credibility to your statements. It is always better if it comes from another person:

> **Example 1:**
> "The Financial Times correspondent said our car looks and goes like a baby Ferrari".

> **Example 2:**
> "The Regulator's report shows us in the top 3, year after year".

Visual Linking:
Showing your audience files, letters, weighty looking documents and the like will create natural jumps in interest as you speak. They link, visually, the words to the item and this is another way of aiding retention.

> **Example:**
> "This file of complaint letters (held up) highlights the major cause of our loss in market share!".

'Selling' Figures:
This can be a very effective way of presenting figures to suit your arguments. The simplest form is a 'reduce or increase to the absurd'.

> **Example:**
> "£500,000 amounts to £10 per person per week (reduce)
> or
> "This is costly. It's £2,500,000 over the next 5 years" (increase).
> or
> "In the 2 minutes since I started speaking, 45 children under the age of 5 will have died from preventable diseases". (increase)

The slightly more complex form is to either reduce or increase and then parallel the amount, ie what would it buy?

> **Example:**
> The BBC licence fee advert –
> "For the cost of a day's licence fee, you can travel 325 yards in a Black Cab!" (reduced to a day's fee and then paralleled).

Examples:
Real life examples bring an element of understanding and illustration of a point better than any other method. How easy would it be to understand this section, if we had not included examples?

Analogies:

The rule we advocate is, if you cannot find an example, use an analogy (a parallel case). The best analogies are domestic ones – they quite literally bring 'home' the point you are making.

> **Example:**
> "We should train all our people up to an advanced level. The basics will then be easy. If you can cook a souffle - you should be able to boil an egg!"

Rhetorical Questions:

In other words, questions that you pose and then immediately answer yourself. Why do rhetorical questions raise audience attention? Because they prompt an audience to think with you. The only warning on these is that you must not leave too long a gap between the question and the answer, or some smart-alec in the audience is likely to throw in his own reply!

Lists of 3:

This is the favourite tool of the politician! Psychologists do not exactly know why, but they do agree that lists of 3 stimulate the human mind. So, if you have two points, find a third, and if you have four points, drop one or merge two together. You should not overplay this but, used correctly, it is a very powerful tool.

> **Example 1:**
> "There are 3 aspects to this. Firstly....secondly....and thirdly...."

> **Example 2:**
> "....freedom to organise secondary strikes against third party employers, other workers, and the general public".

Reiteration of words:

On our courses we ask our audience to name 2 famous speeches. The answers are inevitably, **'We shall fight them on the beaches' (Winston Churchill) and 'I have a dream' (Martin Luther King).** Both of these use reiteration (repeating the same words over and over again) but in different ways. Churchill used what is known as 'listed reiteration', ie ten consecutive sentences each beginning with 'We shall….'. King used 'streamed reiteration', ie he used 'I have a dream' as a theme throughout his speech, separated by his messages – or Vital Points!

What you can also do is tie the last two 'tricks' together and use 'reiterated three's'.

> **Example:**
> "It will be
> - good for employees
> - good for shareholders
> - and good for the company"

Link Sentences:

These are bridging statements which tell an audience what is happening as you move on through the presentation. They are used to create hooks in the mind ready to receive new information. To do this, the sentences need to last between 5 and 7 seconds, which is the time it takes for the minds of the listeners to 'grow' the hook.

> You may recognise this technique from news programmes…
>
> "We're going live now to New York where Andrew Marr is talking to the Secretary General".
>
> And in the example presentation we are using….
>
> "So, having covered what the problems are, let's now move on to look at the solutions".

Recaps:
The conventional reason for recapping (briefly going over what you have said again), is that it reinforces your message. It also allows one other thing to happen – it gives the audience a chance for a mental breather. Since they will already have heard the points before they can allow their attention to wane as you recap, picking up only if they need to listen again to something they may not have understood the first time round. When you move on, however, their attention comes right up again and they are ready for more new information.

Chiasmus:
This is a statement containing two words that are swapped around.
One of the most famous examples is to be found in President Kennedy's inauguration address: **"Ask not what your country can do for you but what you can do for your country."** There are many other examples but to mention one more, which is very apposite for presentation skills: **;To fail to prepare is to prepare to fail."**

Prenomination:
Let the audience know how many key pieces of content you have in a section and highlight the number by prenominating, **ie "There are 2 points/3 points/ 4 points in this section".**

Now you are armed with some techniques, the next question is, how do you apply them to your presentation? This is the difficult part. What you have to do is maintain a conversational style. So, as we have stated earlier, you must not write a script. The best approach is to think of how you would say something to a friend over a drink. This should make you realise that what you do naturally in conversation to explain a point is also the best way to put it across in a presentation.

34 | Help with **High Impact Presentations**

You need to take each A4 sheet or cue card in turn, look at the bullet points and think of the best way to explain them using the 'tricks of the trade'. The easiest way to illustrate this is to use the Vital Point and Bullet Points we gave as an example earlier:

> **What are the Problems?**
> - **Lack of Direction**
> - **Wastage**
> - **Cost**

Remember!

- It is the power of the **message** which is important in a presentation

For the sake of argument, let us assume this point is 2-3 minutes of speech. For the first Bullet Point you could use an analogy and list of 3, a rhetorical question and the start of a streamed reiteration. The second bullet could feature Vivid Language followed by a reiterated list of 3, an example, a third party reference, Visual Link and continue the streamed reiteration. The final Bullet is an obvious candidate for selling figures and the final part of the streamed reiteration. All of these would need link sentences and maybe a recap. Do not be put off by that technical explanation – all will become clear later on. The card might look like this.

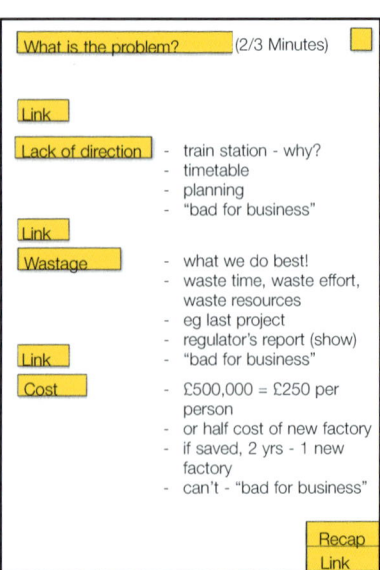

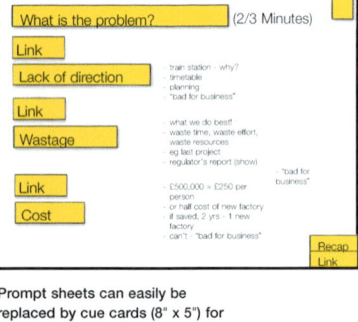

Prompt sheets can easily be replaced by cue cards (8" x 5") for use when speaking to larger audiences.

Figure 10

Divide your speaking time as follows:

- Introduction 10%
- Main Body 80%
- Conclusion 10%

The actual words, spoken conversationally, might sound like this: (explanations of the techniques being used are in brackets):

"Let me start by looking at the first area – What is the Problem? (link). There are 3 main aspects – the first one is our lack of direction (link/list of 3 introduced). Imagine a train station with people waiting for a train to arrive. They don't know if a train is coming. They don't know when a train is coming. They don't even know where that train is going (analogy/reiterated list of 3). Why? (rhetorical question). Because they don't have a timetable. That's the way we're running our business. All of our staff are sitting around, like the people on the station – not really knowing what they're doing. That's because we don't do any planning and that means we lack direction. That is bad for business (analogy concluded/start of streamed reiteration).

The second problem is the wastage involved (link). If you ask me, waste is what we do best! (Vivid Language) We waste time, we waste effort and we waste resources! (reiterated list of 3). Let me give you an example – look at the last project we ran (example). After that, we were publicly criticised by the Regulator in this report (hold up document) for our wastefulness and lack of efficient use of resources (3rd party reference/ visual link). That too is bad for business! (2nd part of streamed reiteration).

The third aspect of the problem is the cost of all this (link). We worked out that it cost us £500,000, That's equivalent to £250 per person per week down the drain. Put another way, it's half the cost of that new factory we want to build (selling figures - reduce and parallel). If we could save on these costs alone, in just 2 years we would be able to build that factory. The fact that we can't do this at the moment is also bad for business (3rd part of streamed reiteration). So, just to recap, the problems are lack of direction, wastage and cost. That covers the problems we face, let me now move on to the second part of the presentation 'How can we solve them?' (recap and link to next vital point).

We are not holding this example up as the greatest piece of speech writing ever – it is purely meant as an explanation of the relationship between what is on the cards (notes) and the words that could be used to put it across. Frankly, the actual words do not matter, it is the power of the **message** which is important in a presentation. The fact that two people may use different words to put across the same points is irrelevant. The important thing is that they speak conversationally, ie they will be putting it across in a way which suits them as individuals. This will mean the presentation sounds fresh and natural.

You would now go on to develop the rest of the Vital Points in exactly the same way – making sure you vary the 'tricks' used as much as possible. The Main Body will then be completed and you can move on to the next stage – putting together the Introduction.

INTRODUCTION (10% OF THE SPEAKING TIME)
There are five parts to this and the idea is to pick out which of the five you are going to use, depending on what is appropriate, given the audience you are presenting to. You then need to decide what order to put them in as this can obviously vary. We will outline the parts and then give an example.

SELF/BACKGROUND:
Simple enough, but remember it is to establish credibility in your subject, not just to let them know who you are.

'GRABBER':
This is the attention grabber – the technique which is designed to kill the 'morbidity' we mentioned earlier in this chapter.

There are a number of ways you can do this:

Humour:
Breaks the ice, gives the impression that the presentation may be fun to listen to. The tests for humour are: firstly, is it appropriate to the subject? Secondly, will it matter if the audience does not laugh? Thirdly, are you comfortable with trying to deliver humour in the first place?

Drama:
A high risk – high return strategy. Examples would be: Experiments, demonstrations, dramatic gestures, dramatic statements.

WIIFM:
Literally "What's in it for me" (the 'me' refers to the audience of course).

Controversy:
Deliberate use of a statement intended to provoke the audience to think about your topic. (See later example).

Quotations:
Everybody likes a good quote. Make sure it is relevant to the topic.
We always advise setting up a quotes file, gathered from newspapers, magazines, letters, reports, etc, rather than simply resorting to a dictionary of quotes. The reason is that the quotes may be less well-known and therefore more impactful.

Stories:
The same principle applies as for quotations. Anecdotes work wonders for attention levels. The test again is relevance to the topic.

STATE THE AIM:
Nobody likes hidden agendas in presentations.

Telling the audience the aim (which we decided in Chapter 2) Clarifies the purpose of them being there and demonstrates that you have thought it through. Try to ensure that it flows naturally from the 'grabber'.

INTRODUCE THE TITLE OF THE PRESENTATION:
Formal presentations should have titles. Try to make them interesting – play with the imagination of the audience rather than having bland report-style titles. For example, 'The important of Sugar in our lives' would be far better as 'Sugar – it can't be beat!'. Another example is the one used in Figure 11. Your title should be visually displayed on an overhead, slide or flipchart.

THE FORMAT:

Deal with 3 things here. Tell them how long the Presentation will last, followed by stating all the Vital Points you will cover and then what you intend to do about questions from them. Try to persuade them to leave questions until the end of the presentation - that way you will maintain control.

You need to decide which of the above 5 points you are going to use, in what order, and then put together a card along the same lines as the Main Body cards, in terms of layout. Here is a typical example of an Introduction for a presentation to a Board of Directors, demonstrating all 5 parts: Once again, using explanation of the techniques in brackets where necessary, the words spoken would be something like this:

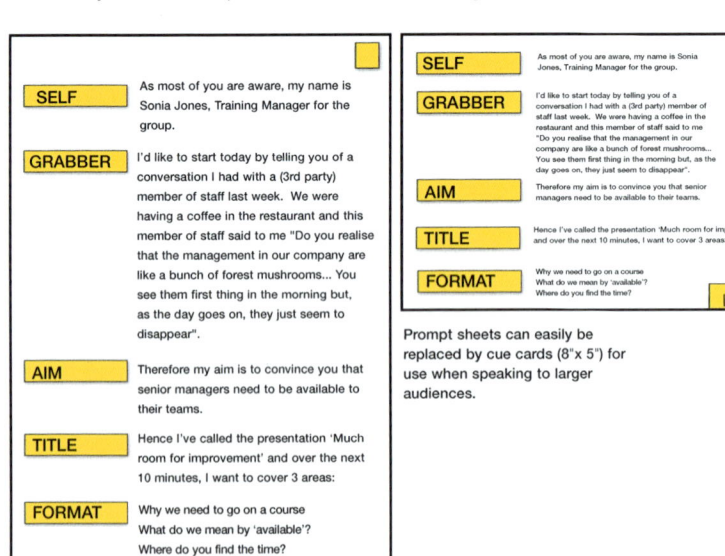

SELF	As most of you are aware, my name is Sonia Jones, Training Manager for the group.
GRABBER	I'd like to start today by telling you of a conversation I had with a (3rd party) member of staff last week. We were having a coffee in the restaurant and this member of staff said to me "Do you realise that the management in our company are like a bunch of forest mushrooms... You see them first thing in the morning but, as the day goes on, they just seem to disappear".
AIM	Therefore my aim is to convince you that senior managers need to be available to their teams.
TITLE	Hence I've called the presentation 'Much room for improvement' and over the next 10 minutes, I want to cover 3 areas:
FORMAT	Why we need to go on a course What do we mean by 'available'? Where do you find the time?

Link

SELF	As most of you are aware, my name is Sonia Jones, Training Manager for the group.
GRABBER	I'd like to start today by telling you of a conversation I had with a (3rd party) member of staff last week. We were having a coffee in the restaurant and this member of staff said to me "Do you realise that the management in our company are like a bunch of forest mushrooms... You see them first thing in the morning but, as the day goes on, they just seem to disappear".
AIM	Therefore my aim is to convince you that senior managers need to be available to their teams.
TITLE	Hence I've called the presentation 'Much room for improvement' and over the next 10 minutes, I want to cover 3 areas:
FORMAT	Why we need to go on a course What do we mean by 'available'? Where do you find the time?

Link

Prompt sheets can easily be replaced by cue cards (8"x 5") for use when speaking to larger audiences.

Figure 11

So let's start by taking the first area.

CONCLUSION (10% OF THE SPEAKING TIME)

You will remember that, in Chapter 2, we highlighted 2 types of Aim statement to express the learning outcome of the presentation. Your choice of Aim then will now affect your choice of conclusion because each Aim needs a different way of finishing the presentation.

If your Aim is 'to give an understanding of.....', you should use a 2-part conclusion, ie:

- Summarise each Vital Point
- Restate the Aim

This is a very simple way of driving home your points and ensuring that the audience will have an understanding of what you have said. It is purely a summary of the Bullet Points under each Vital Point. The example below should be self-explanatory:

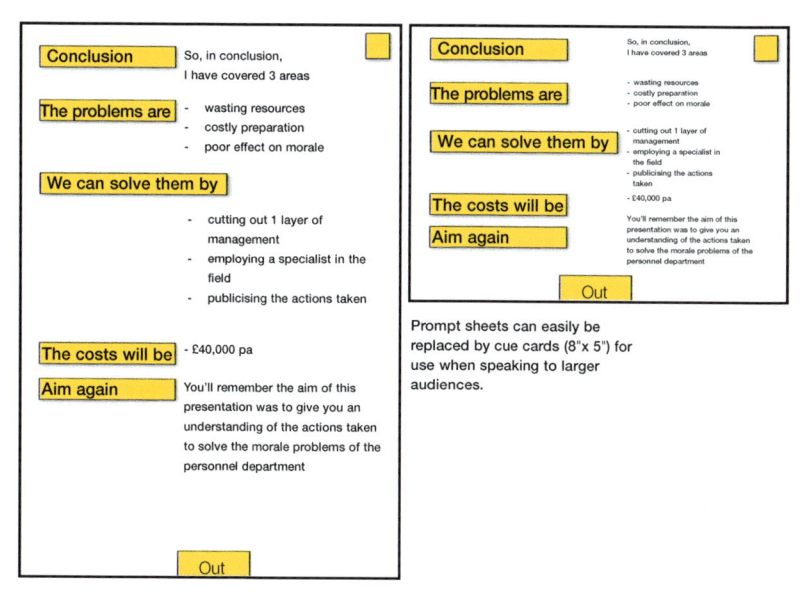

Prompt sheets can easily be replaced by cue cards (8"x 5") for use when speaking to larger audiences.

Figure 12

You will notice a box at the bottom of the card – 'OUT'. This is to remind the speaker to close with an 'out sentence'. The best one to use is:

"That concludes my presentation. If you have any questions, I'd be pleased to answer them."

Or – if there is no need/time for questions:

"That concludes my presentation. Thank you for listening".

Incidentally, restating the Aim at the end is done to remind the audience of the whole point of the presentation and an effective way of rounding off.

The other sort of conclusion is used **when your Aim was 'to convince…'**. It is a 4-part close and is, necessarily, more powerful than the 2-part close. It uses a mixture of common sense and psychology. The 4 parts are:

- **Ask for action**
- **Restate why/the benefits**
- **Refer back to the 'grabber'**
- **Leave them with a final thought**

Parts 1 and 2 are fairly logical – effectively it is asking for something and reminding them why they should do it. Part 3 – referring back to the 'grabber' – may need explanation. The reason this is done is to give the audience a feeling of having completed a journey – of coming full circle to the beginning again. Psychologists in America have found that this creates a feeling of comfort and achievement. Many of the latest films and videos use a similar technique by returning to a scene which appeared at the start of the film, before they finish the story off. Since the 'grabber' is likely to be the only thing the audience will remember of the start, it is used to do the same job.

Part 4 – the 'final thought' – provides an opportunity to leave the audience with something to think about. This should be used as a method of reinforcement. In other words, a way of hammering home the need to do whatever it is that you are asking for. Once again, we will illustrate this by an example card, which is self-explanatory, using the same subject featured in our example Introduction:

Help with **High Impact Presentations** | 41

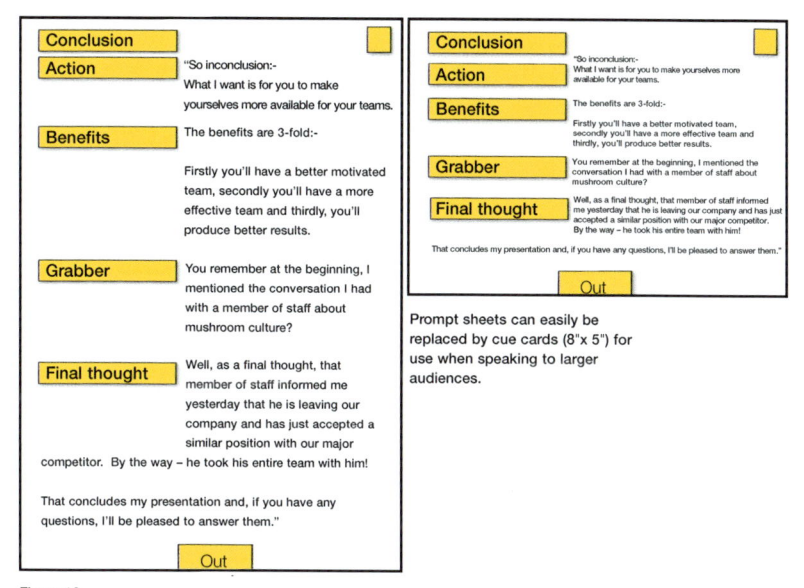

Conclusion	
Action	"So inconclusion:- What I want is for you to make yourselves more available for your teams.
Benefits	The benefits are 3-fold:-
	Firstly you'll have a better motivated team, secondly you'll have a more effective team and thirdly, you'll produce better results.
Grabber	You remember at the beginning, I mentioned the conversation I had with a member of staff about mushroom culture?
Final thought	Well, as a final thought, that member of staff informed me yesterday that he is leaving our company and has just accepted a similar position with our major competitor. By the way – he took his entire team with him!
	That concludes my presentation and, if you have any questions, I'll be pleased to answer them."
Out	

Conclusion	
Action	"So inconclusion:- What I want is for you to make yourselves more available for your teams.
Benefits	The benefits are 3-fold:- Firstly you'll have a better motivated team, secondly you'll have a more effective team and thirdly, you'll produce better results.
Grabber	You remember at the beginning, I mentioned the conversation I had with a member of staff about mushroom culture?
Final thought	Well, as a final thought, that member of staff informed me yesterday that he is leaving our company and has just accepted a similar position with our major competitor. By the way – he took his entire team with him!
That concludes my presentation and, if you have any questions, I'll be pleased to answer them."	
Out	

Prompt sheets can easily be replaced by cue cards (8"x 5") for use when speaking to larger audiences.

Figure 13

A variation on this theme is to use a technique known as the 'split grabber'. This is based on using the 'story' grabber option and only works if it is possible to divide the story into 2 parts (split the grabber). You tell the first half of your story in the Introduction as your grabber. In the Conclusion, you ask for action and restate the benefits as before; then retell the first half of the story to remind them. Then instead of using a separate final thought, you finish the story off. A good link line for this is: "What I didn't tell you at the start was that….". This is the most powerful variation of the technique of all and is used widely, both in documentaries and films.

So, at this stage we have now put together all 3 parts of the presentation – the Main Body, followed by the Introduction and the Conclusion. The next question is, how do we use the voice to ensure that it matches the interest and power of the message we have just designed? That takes us on to 'How it is said – Part 2':

PART 2 (Use of the Voice)

A good exercise to start with is to imagine you are a radio presenter delivering the gardening programme. Record yourself reading the following script and time it as you do so:

> "One thing I can advise, keep ants under control. They guard and milk greenfly and have even been known to carry them from plant to plant. Next month is an ideal time to plant an evergreen hedge so this month prepare the site by digging a trench three feet wide by one spade deep. And then dig the bottom of the trench, forking in as much organic material as you can get – mushroom compost, rotten manure, adding some of the same compost to the top soil whilst filling in the trench."

Pausing and use of emphasis

forces a slower overall delivery, allows presenters to catch their breath and therefore restores normal modulation.

How long did you take? The average person takes between 26 and 30 seconds. The overall effect is usually pretty dull as the delivery sounds flat and lacking in impact. When trained speakers deliver the same script, they will take about 42 seconds, ie 12-16 seconds longer. They will give it life and make it sound meaningful. The question is, how? The answer is a combination of 5 things:

PAUSES

Silence is golden on occasions. Pauses are designed into a speech or presentation and are usually indicated like this (PAUSE). This instructs the speaker to stop speaking **and maintain eye contact with the audience** whilst counting to 3. This will create a 2-second pause in speech and 4 benefits;

2 for the speaker:

1. Gather thoughts, think about the next point
2. Draw a breath

And 2 for the audience:

1. Silence raises their attention levels
2. Allows them to absorb the last point

> <u>twenty-six</u> (1 second)
> **<u>million</u> (1 second)**
> <u>pounds</u> (1 second)

VARIATION IN PACE OF DELIVERY

The trick here is to inject sudden bursts of speed to convey a sense of urgency and enthusiasm, countered by use of emphasis (see below). This will create almost a 'stop-start' rhythm to your voice and is always a feature of good speakers. The faster pace is normally induced quite naturally – by nerves! (hence the faster delivery of the gardening text by most people).

Give your presentation life with:

- Pauses
- Pace changes
- Emphasis
- Voice Modulation
- Contrasts and mood changes

EMPHASIS

There is a very effective way to self-teach this. The normal method used is to identify points for emphasis (eg large numbers, important points you want to stress, certain individual words to add impact) and script them out.
For example, '£26m' would become 'Profits – 26 million pounds'. Then add single underlining on each part to denote the need to take **one second** per word, ie '26 million pounds'. Decide if there needs to be a 'key emphasis point' and double underline that part. Our example would need key emphasis on the word 'million', ie '<u>26</u> <u><u>million</u></u> <u>pounds</u>'.

VOICE MODULATION

This is what most people describe as 'going up and down'; sometimes using high pitch and other times using low pitch sounds. The definition of the word 'monotonous' is 'of one tone' and the effect is, as we all know, a boring voice. In fact, modulation is natural to most people in every day conversation. What happens when they present however is that they speed up their speech rate, cannot therefore breath properly, and so crush or flatten out their normal modulation. Pausing and use of emphasis forces a slower overall delivery, allows presenters to catch their breath and therefore restores normal modulation. In short, lack of modulation is merely a by-product of speaking too quickly.

CONTRASTS AND MOOD CHANGES

Sometimes referred to as 'light and dark' in the voice. Try to think about the tone of the message. If it is serious – speak loudly and be serious about it. If it is something you want your audience to ponder, try speaking quietly at that point – their attention will **shoot** up! Similarly, if you want to inject movement onto a more salient point – speed up and lighten your tone.

Now read, time and record the gardening script again. This time try to use the techniques described and you should end up taking 42 seconds **and** sound very much more impactful.

> "One thing I <u>can</u> advise (PAUSE) keep <u>ants</u> under control. They guard and milk greenfly and have <u>even</u> been known to carry them from plant to plant (PAUSE). <u>Next</u> month is an <u>ideal</u> time to plant an evergreen hedge, <u>so</u> <u>this month</u> prepare the site by digging a trench three feet wide by <u>one spade deep</u> and then (PAUSE) dig the <u>bottom</u> of the trench, forking in as much <u>organic material</u> as you can get – <u>peat, mushroom compost, rotten manure,</u> adding some of this <u>same</u> compost to the top soil, whilst filling in the trench."

If you are not satisfied with how you sound the first time, keep reading it until it becomes natural.

Another exercise we recommend to help with this, is to record and transcribe one minute's worth of a short story being read by an actor/actress on Radio 4. Then record yourself reading it, whilst trying to mimic the way you heard them read it. The results are usually startling.

So, by now you should have a message which is well-designed and impactful and some idea of how to use your voice to deliver it correctly. You can now put pauses and emphasis lines on your cards which will help in this process. Emphasis lines are obviously a matter of choice, depending on your message. We recommend that you insert pauses according to the following list:

Introduction
- After the 'grabber'
- After the title
- Before the link to the Main Body

Main Body
- Before you link onto a new Vital Point
- Where needed for impact in each Vital Point
- Before the words: "So, in conclusion…"

Conclusion (2 Part)
- After the summary of Vital Points
- Before the 'OUT'

Conclusion (4 Part)
- Before the final thought
- Before the 'OUT'

The next decision is how to visually support your presentation. That takes us on to the use of Visual Aids.

The Ford Motor Company

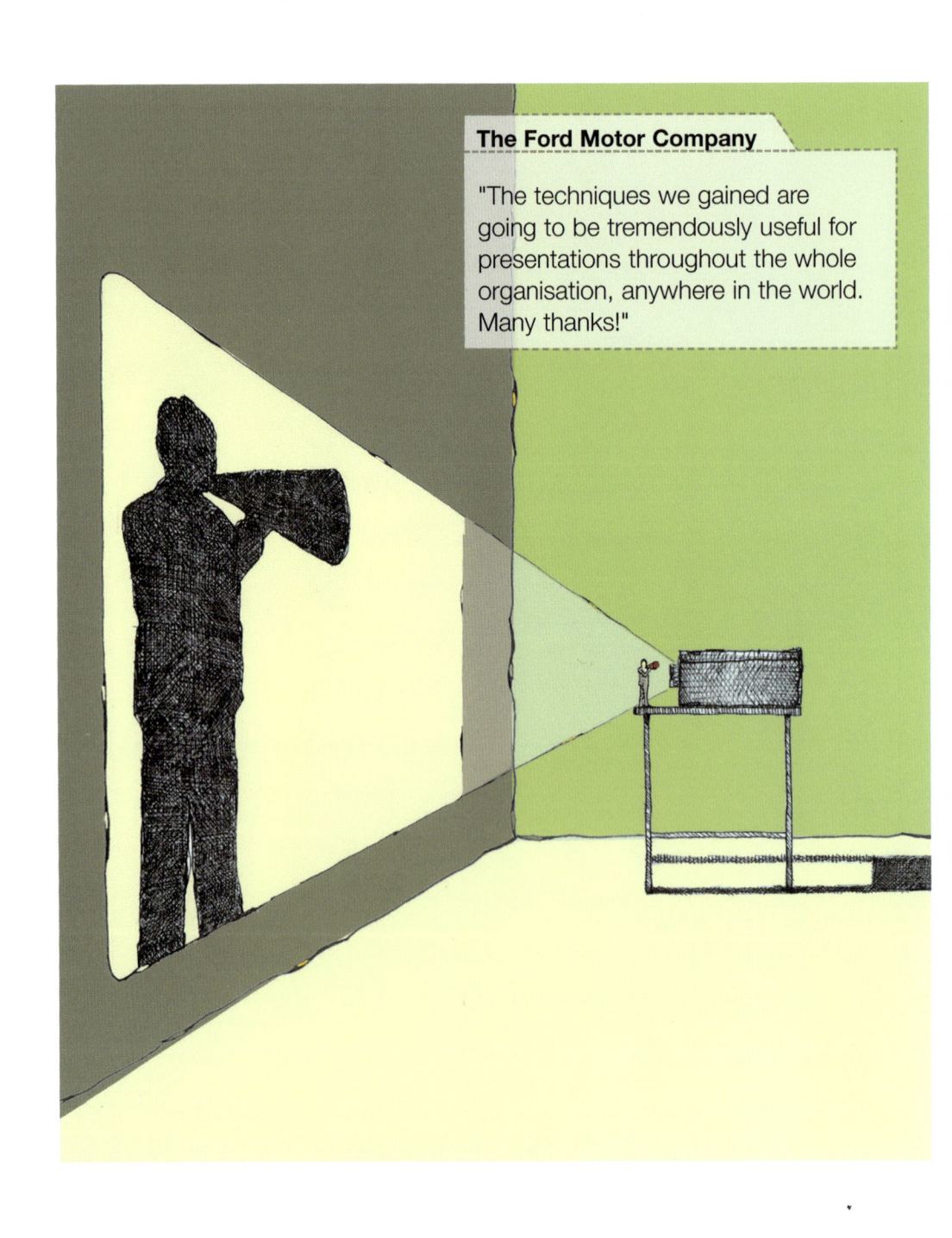

"The techniques we gained are going to be tremendously useful for presentations throughout the whole organisation, anywhere in the world. Many thanks!"

Chapter 4
Visual Aids (12%)

You will recall that this is 12% of the impression made during a presentation. This may seem like a low figure. It is. The reason is that for the majority of the time, audiences are looking at **you** – the presenter – and we will be dealing with this aspect in the next chapter – on Body Language.

Help your audience further understand your message with:

- Data Projections
- Models
- Flipcharts
- Video

Visual Aids can accurately be defined as 'something which helps an audience further to understand your message, by means of simple visual stimulus'. In other words, a presentation should consist of a speaker, **backed by visual aids**, not the other way around.

The 5 general hints to bear in mind are:

- **You** are the primary visual aid, as mentioned before. So, image, dress, appearance are all extremely important when you present.
- Design your message first. Then spread your speaker notes out and apply the definition given above for visual aids to decide what **they** will need to help **them** 'further understand' your message.
- Remember the word 'visual'. Audiences like to see pictures, items, cartoons, diagrams, simple charts, graphs and the like. They do not respond well to text. TRY TO KEEP WORDS OFF YOUR VISUAL AIDS!
- Apply the 'KISS' test (Keep It Simple, Stupid). Audiences **will not** take in too much detail from over-crowded, complicated visuals. What may be acceptable for reading in a publication or handout is rarely adequate as a visual aid in a presentation.
- Do not talk to your visual aid. Remember that screens, flipcharts, items, slides – whatever you are using – **never** want to hear your presentation. Your **audience** might though!

With those general tips in mind, we can now examine the various forms of visual aid equipment and their suggested usage.

DATA PROJECTORS & POWERPOINT
Increasingly popular and perceived to be 'professional' and 'slick', they can be dangerous if you follow the fixed formats. These encourage the use of bullet points and should be avoided. Start with the 'blank' slide format and develop your own graphics (see point 3, page 45).

ACTUAL ITEMS AND MODELS
Quite simply, the best! Holding up even the most basic items for the audience to see causes huge leaps in their attention levels. They bring a natural interest and presence of their own. Avoid handing them round during the presentation – you lose control. This applies to paperwork as well – leave it to the end.

FLIPCHARTS
Much maligned for being 'unprofessional'. Nowadays however they can be produced inexpensively on a machine which converts A4 to A1 flipchart size). So any images which a personal computer can produce can be displayed on a flipchart. We recommend that the Title, together with a list of Vital Points underneath, is put on the flipchart. This provides a good backdrop for the audience, enabling them to have a constant frame of reference for what point you are covering, what you have already covered, and what is left. By using this, in conjunction with 'link sentences' and 'general gesturing', you can literally guide the audience through your presentation. This simple use of a visual aid has been shown to increase audiences' retention by up to 15%.

VIDEOS

The one thing videos do which no other visual equipment can is bring outside reality into the room in a moving format. On our courses, for example, how else could we show different speakers in action? There are 3 very good tests when contemplating the use of a video clip:

- Is it totally relevant and up-to-date?
- No more than 5 minutes long at a time? Any more than this and audiences switch to 'TV watching' mode which is associated with relaxation and leisure!
- Can it be used without sound? If possible, try doing this. **You** can then do the talking over the pictures and that way maintain continuity and control. Otherwise, you risk competing with a professional voice-over!

Short, sharp clips at the start, middle or end (or even at all 3 points) of your presentation will work wonders, provided the 3 tests above are implemented.

We advocate a mixed media approach; in other words, do not be afraid of using more than one type of visual aid during a presentation. It will add greatly to the interest from an audience's point of view. Remember, the definition of a visual aid given at the start of this chapter, apply it constantly to your intended material and you will not go far wrong.

Dresdner Kleinwort Wasserstein

"I am convinced that the skills and techniques that I learnt on the course contributed significantly to the overall success of our pitch."

Chapter 5
Body Language (30%)

As the audience analysis suggests, this is a very important part of the presentation. Audiences are all very capable of analysing your body language subconsciously – without being very aware of it. The impression made is instant and, more often than not, can contradict the positive message you have designed and are desperately trying to put across. You need therefore to be very aware of the body language you exhibit, from the moment you stand up until the time you sit down again after the presentation. In short, you need **positive words, matched by positive body language.** This chapter is in 2 sections: firstly, it will deal with 'positive' body language (what to do) and secondly, 'negative' body language (what not to do).

Remember!

- The impression made is instant

Section 1 – Positive Body Language

The first thing you need to be aware of is that audiences are very conscious of zones – distances we all use between each other in different circumstances. The zone used for presentations is known as the 'Public Zone' and is defined as 7 feet plus. This means that you should stand at least 7 feet away from the nearest member of the audience – the bigger the audience, the further away you will be. Stand any closer and you will antagonise those affected, as described in Section 2 of this chapter.
This fact has obvious connotations for room and equipment layout and we will mention more about this in the next chapter.
Once you have made sure you are operating in the correct zone, there are 2 further aspects of positive body language you need to be aware of: what to do with your eyes and what to do with the rest of your body.

Figure 14

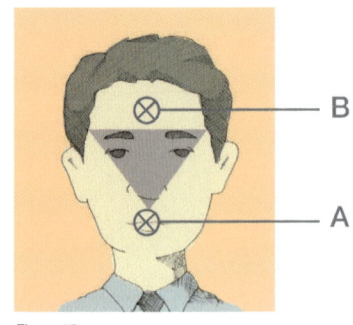

Figure 15

Eyes:

Everyone knows that a presenter needs to have eye contact with his/her audience. Most people are not aware however of just how sensitive audiences are to this. Figure 14 shows the area of the face which presenters should aim for when looking at their audience.

Anywhere in the shaded triangular area will be positive eye contact. You do not therefore need to look directly into a person's eyes. We tell the people we train to imagine a 'traffic sign' on the face of each audience member and scan in that area.

If you allow your eyes to fix on anywhere else on the face, you will create negative eye contact. Figure 15 explains this effect.

Position A depicts what is know as the 'intimate gaze'. In other words, by moving literally 1 inch downwards outside the triangle, you are entering the 'intimate zone' of another person. Their typical reaction will be to describe this in a variety of ways: "uncomfortable", "staring at me", "you look shifty!". They will not know what is causing the effect, it is purely a subconscious reaction, as mentioned earlier. Position B shows a 'dominant gaze'. This is only 2 inches above the eyebrows. The reaction to this will be to describe you as: "aloof", "arrogant", "staring through me", "talking down to me".

Experiment with either of these negative eye contact positions on people you know and they will readily confirm the reactions described here. The important point for eye contact is clear – STAY IN THE TRIANGULAR AREA SHOWN IN FIGURE 14!

Rest of your body:
We will take legs and feet first. Try to inject **movement** as you speak. This creates natural interest as the audience will need to shift their gaze to follow you, rather than staring at you in one position all the time. The technique we use for this is known as the 'actor's glide'. Whilst the rules are simple to explain, the execution of it is a different matter! Never allow your shoulders to turn more than 30 degrees towards the direction you wish to move. This creates an instant restriction. You will not be able to walk as you would normally, without looking very odd indeed! So, the legs should cross in front of each other as your 'crab' sideways. It is important to do this very slowly (a pace every 1 or 2 seconds). This will create the 'glide' we referred to above. Do not take too many steps at a time, you only need to move 3 or 4 feet to create the effect. The reason to try this is that, when done properly, it will make you look very confident and in control – which is a very powerful and positive message to deliver, simply by moving a certain way! We suggest that you allow yourself to be choreographed by the Link sentences, ie as you verbally move on, physically move on as well. It is important not to move constantly as this will irritate the audience, so by allowing the structure of the presentation to dictate movement, you can easily avoid this pitfall.

Having chosen your spot, so to speak, what then? How should you stand? The answer is simple. You should stand with your feet about 3 inches apart and the weight balanced evenly on each leg. (Figure 16 shows this).

The second aspect to consider under the 'rest of body language' section, is what to do with your arms and hands. The key to success here is to do what you do normally. When, for example, you are standing talking to colleagues in a bar, you do not even think about arm or hand movements. You allow them to work with you as you converse. The same rule applies in presentations, with a minor adjustment. When presenting, it is important to move your hands away from your body regularly. Keeping the arms parallel to the ground, show the palms of the hands and then return them to a position in front of you again (see Figure 16). This displays openness, confidence and is an embracing gesture towards your audience.

Figure 16

So, to summarise positive body language:

> - Stand at least 7 feet away
> - Eye contact only in the triangle shape shown in Figure 14
> - Move using the 'actor's glide'
> - When standing still – feet 3 inches apart, weight evenly balanced
> - Keep arms parallel to the ground at all times
> - Occasionally move arms away from body and show palms of the hands

Section 2 – Negative Body Language

There are 2 kinds of negative body language – 'negative passive' and 'negative aggressive':

Negative Passive (Figure 17):
This will portray lack of confidence, lack of preparation and lack of belief in your message!

The classic symptoms are shown in the diagram to the right.

Figure 17

Figure 18

Even if your message is clear and your voice authoratitive, you will still come across as negative if you show any of these symptoms.

- Standing with your weight on one leg in an unbalanced stance
- Arms held together and low across the body to 'protect' yourself
- Eye contact darting from one member of the audience to another, looking down in the 'intimate zone' described earlier

Even worse is negative aggressive (Figure 18).
This will portray arrogance, close-mindedness, and a domineering attitude.

The classic symptoms of this behaviour are:
It should be obvious that this behaviour will score no points at all as far as an audience is concerned!

- Eye contact on one or two of the audience, using the 'dominant' gaze described earlier
- A hard, glaring, unsmiling face with the chin held high
- Hands on hips (one or both)
- Constant intrusion **inside** the 7 feel zone, as you attempt to hammer home your points

In summary, it is essential to match your positive words and delivery with a positive body language to ensure you come across well. Remember that you only need one aspect of any of the negative body language described to detract from your performance. Perfecting body language so that it becomes second-nature is purely a matter of practice, be it in front of a mirror or by being videoed. This way you can correct errors as they occur and programme your subconscious to instruct your body to behave as you would wish.

BP

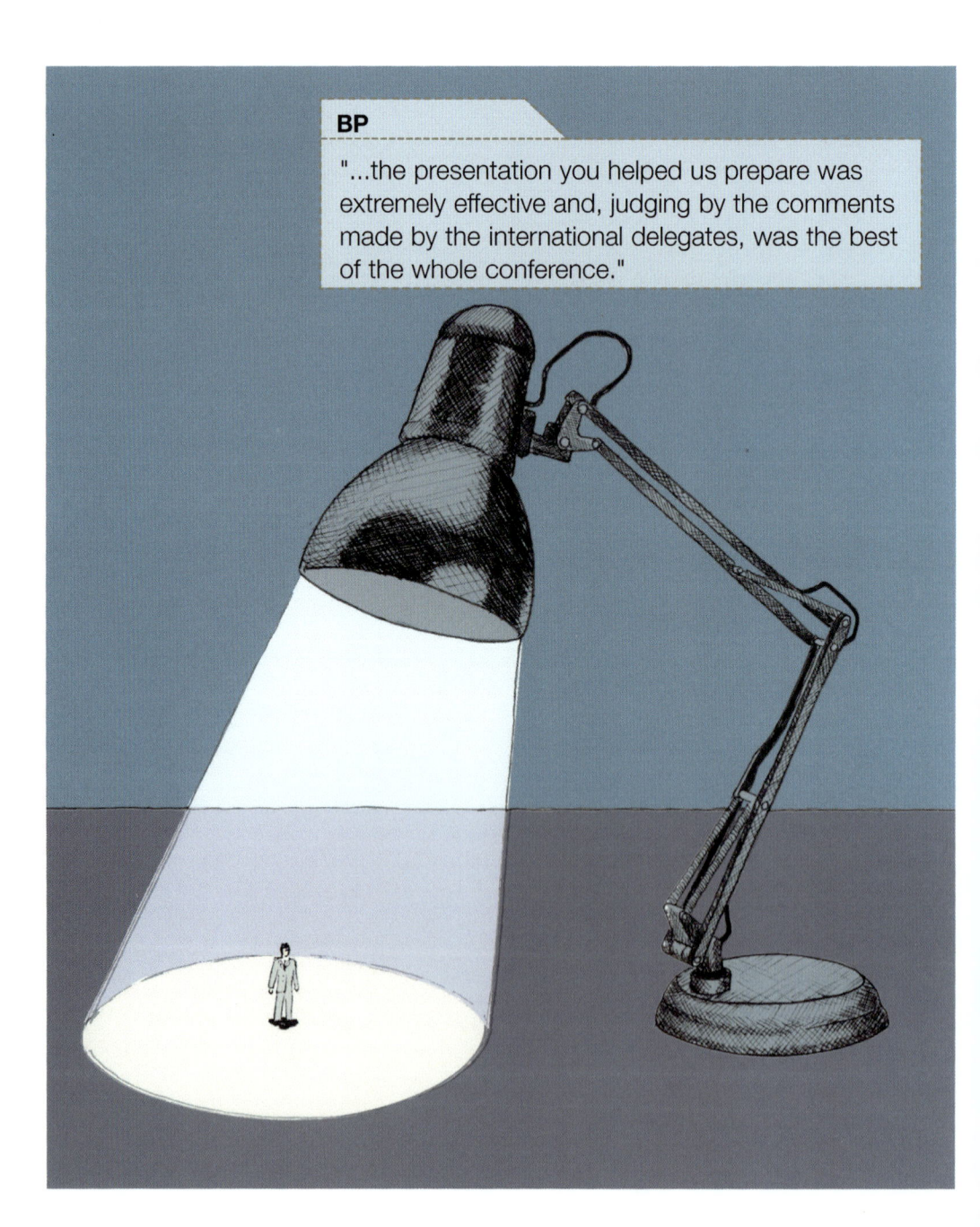

"...the presentation you helped us prepare was extremely effective and, judging by the comments made by the international delegates, was the best of the whole conference."

Chapter 6
'Personal' Concerns

This chapter aims to deal with the sort of questions we are constantly asked on our courses, reflecting what we call 'personal concerns'.

How do I overcome nerves/gain confidence?

Key concerns:
- Nerves
- Eye Contact
- Enthusiasm
- Positioning
- Timing

The first thing to realise is that you are not alone! A survey in the USA showed speaking in public as the thing people feared most in life. Death was number 7 on the list!

There is a lot of well documented and conflicting advice on how to overcome nerves. In our experience nerves are natural – they provide the 'edge' that a person needs in order to perform. This point is certainly borne out by people who speak in public regularly. A far more relevant question therefore is, what do these people do to control nerves when speaking? There are 3 ways you can control and contain your nerves:

i) Interpret the physical symptoms correctly

When you speak in public, 4 symptoms occur. Firstly, your temperature increases – you will notice perhaps that your palms start to sweat. Secondly, adrenaline is pumped into your bloodstream – this will cause some people to shake! Thirdly, your respiration rate increases – this results in a feeling of panic and causes some people to stumble over their words. Finally, you will start to consume sugar – this has the effect of drying your mouth out.

Put all of the above together and it is easy to see why most people interpret them as signs of fear. They are not. Surveys conducted, for example, on Olympic athletes before they compete, have found the same

4 symptoms happen to **them**. And yet they go out and win gold medals whilst, in a different circumstance, people see these physical symptoms as signs of fear. In fact, they are manifestations of the fact that a person is 'tooled up' to perform. They are signs that you do have the necessary 'edge'. The time to panic is when you do not have them!

So, interpreting these things correctly and understanding why they happen, is one way to control your feeling of nerves.

ii) The 3 'P's!

'Proper Preparation and Practice'. The previous chapters have dealt with preparing properly, in other words, putting together a high-impact presentation which has a chance of being interesting and of satisfying the audience needs. The third 'P' – Practice - cannot be over stressed. The number of times we hear people making excuses for not having rehearsed their presentations due to 'lack of time' is amazing. These people seem to think that rehearsals are only something professionals do. The logic of this is beyond us! We recommend a **minimum** of 4 rehearsals prior to presenting, using 'visualisation' techniques. This simply means going through the presentation in your head – imagining that you are doing it for real in front of an audience. This technique allows even the hard-pressed to find time for rehearsals. Travelling to and from meetings or work, eating lunch or dinner, last thing at night, even whilst bathing in the morning – these are **all** opportunities you can use to rehearse. The benefit of this method is that you are effectively 'programming' the brain to perform the way you want to on the day. It is a well-proven and highly effective way to rehearse, especially when under pressure of time.

iii) Concentrate on the message, NOT the audience!

This may seem like a complete contradiction of everything we have said so far. It is not. You should worry about audiences whilst preparing, not when presenting. The reason for this is that if you try to concentrate on how the audience is reacting during your presentation, you are bound to suffer severe nerves. The moment you ask yourself the fatal question, "How am I doing?", you are in trouble. Audiences are complex enough and your self-assessment 'on hoof' will add nothing at all to your performance; if anything, it will detract from it. So, by concentrating on your **message**, ie "What I am trying to say about….", you will focus your mind on the task in hand. It is a well-known fact that the human mind, wonderful thought it may be, cannot concentrate on more than one major task at a time. When skiing, for example, you cannot think about work or domestic problems as well. All you have in your head is staying upright/negotiating the next turn etc. The same applies to presenting – concentrating on the message is a major task. Do that effectively and you will find that you will not worry about audiences, or suffer from nerves!

Is there a way of breathing which will help me?
Yes! You need to breathe much more deeply than normal. As an exercise to help with this, try taking a large breath whilst holding the bottom of your ribcage with your hands on each side of your back (rather like the diagram in Figure 18). They should move outwards as the air reaches the bottom of your lungs and pushes against the ribcage. Now try to control your exhalation so that you can breathe out at a steady rate for 25-30 seconds. Practice this until you can do it easily. You will then know how much breath you need whilst presenting. This will give you more volume and power **and** it will also help to control your feeling of nervousness, brought on by the respiration rate increase described earlier in 1 (i).

How do I appear enthusiastic when I don't feel it?
It is difficult to feel enthusiastic when under pressure. What you **can** do is **portray** enthusiasm, which is all that matters.

Enthusiasm is portrayed by a combination of 4 things:

- Smiling where appropriate
- Letting your hands work with you, as described in the chapter on Body Language
- Speaking with a fast pace on occasion (see Chapter 3 – Using the Voice)
- Maintaining eye contact with the audience (see Body Language)

Remove any one of these and you will not appear enthusiastic. Remember that enthusiasm is extremely infectious – if you have it, the audience has it as well. If you do not have it – neither will they!

How long should I spend looking at each individual in the audience?
You should not really worry too much about this – but as a rough guide, 2 seconds each. What is more important is to scan round at everyone so that you do not leave any person out. Avoid also, looking at one person more than the others! This regularly happens if you spot a friendly, smiling face or are conscious of a decision maker/important person.

How should I set the room up?
Most of the time there is very little scope for manoeuvre. If there is , we suggest an open seating arrangement – usually an 'n' shape. Allow, if possible, **at least** 10 feet from the nearest seat to the visual aid equipment, so as to provide a 'stage area' for you to move in. Try to make sure the projector does not block out part of the screen from where the audience is sitting – keep the body of the machine as low as possible. Test each seat individually to get a feel for the view the audience will have. Check temperature and lighting levels, sun streaming through windows, need for blinds or curtains to be drawn, clarity and focus of projection on screens etc. In short, it comes down to thinking audience again and remembering that it is the presenter's job to arrange these things!

How do I ensure that I don't overrun?
You can normally tackle this at design stage, using the 10/80/10 rule we discussed in Chapter 3. This can be checked and adjusted further during done of your rehearsals by timing your run-through and either taking some detail out, or expanding a point if you find you are under time. Audiences will mentally allow for a 10% leeway. In other words, a stated '10 minute' presentation should be finished by minute 11 at the latest or they will become restless. Timing yourself **during** the presentation is all very well in theory. In reality, you have enough to worry about the it is strange how unable you are to work it out from the watch or clock on the table in front of you, as you are speaking! It is all down to preparation and rehearsal.

Remember!
Before the presentation, rehearse at least 4 times.

Chapter 7
Summary and 15 Point Guideline

This final section is intended to provide a fast reference check-off list of all the actions required in order to design a presentation in the future. For detail, refer to the relevant pages given in brackets. IT IS IMPORTANT NOT TO DEVIATE FROM THE LIST, BUT TO DO WHAT IS SUGGESTED **IN THE ORDER GIVEN.**

Putting the presentation together – 15 point plan:

1. Decide which character type your audience is: Emotive, Directive, Reflective, Supportive or a mix (Pages 24-29)

2. Decide your Aim. Either "To give you an understanding or...." or "To convince you...." (Page 24)

3. Read your Aim out to people of the **same character type** as your intended audience and ask them to give you the Vital Points (page 29)

4. Put each Vital Point on an A4 sheet (or 8" x 5" card) in a box at the top (Page 32)

5. Arrange Vital Points into a sequence according to order of importance **to the audience**, ie 'shuffle' and number the speaker notes (Page 39)

6. Decide the Bullet Points for each Vital Point. Put in boxes down left hand side of notes, allowing space in between each. Remember they are **answers** (Page 46).

7. Apply the "so what?" test as applicable to each answer.

8. Allocate speaking time to each Vital Point, ie take **total** length of presentation, proportion according to the 10/80/10 rule and allocate minutes to each Vital Point. Allow 2 mins for every 3 bullet points. (Pages 37-40)

9. Work through each point, deciding which 'Tricks of the Trade' to use to Illustrate each bullet point. Write prompts on the speaker notes to remind you of the ideas.

> **Tricks of the Trade: (Pages 39-43)**
>
> - Vivid Language
> - Referring to 3rd parties
> - Visual Linking
> - Selling Figures
> - Examples
> - Analogies
> - Rhetorical Questions
> - Lists of 3
> - Reiteration of words
> - Links
> - Recaps
> - Chiasmus
> - Prenomination

10. Design Introduction and choosing from 5 parts ie: (Pages 48-50)

> (i)   Self/background
> (ii) 'Grabber' – humour/drama/ controversy/quotation or story
> (iii) Aim statement
> (iv) Title
> (v)   Length of presentation, list of Vital Points, "...questions at end". Put on speaker notes

11. Design Conclusion. (Pages 51-54)
    Remember there are 2 types, depending on your choice of Aim:

    If Aim was 'to give you an understanding of...."

    - **Summarise each Vital Point**
    - **Remind audiences of your Aim**

    If Aim was "to convince you...."

    - **Ask for action**
    - **Restate benefits (preferably 3!)**
    - **Refer back to 'grabber'**
    - **Leave them with a final thought**

    Add the 'OUT' statement, ie "That concludes my presentation. If you have any questions, I'd be pleased to answer them."
    Put on speaker notes

12. Put (PAUSE) on speaker notes in places needed (Page 55)

13. Put emphasis lines on speaker notes where needed (Page 55)

14. Decide and design the Visual Aids required and note on speaker notes as appropriate. (Pages 59-61)

15. Rehearse at least 4 times

    And... **GOOD LUCK!**

Printed in Great Britain
by Amazon